# ROAM

Crab Orchard Series in Poetry

*Open Competition Award*

# ROAM

Susan B. A. Somers-Willett

*Crab Orchard Review*

*&*

Southern Illinois University Press

CARBONDALE

All rights reserved

Printed in the United States of America

09   08   07   06   4   3   2   1

The Crab Orchard Series in Poetry is a joint publishing venture of Southern Illinois University Press and *Crab Orchard Review*. This series has been made possible by the generous support of the Office of the President of Southern Illinois University and the Office of the Vice Chancellor for Academic Affairs and Provost at Southern Illinois University Carbondale.

**Crab Orchard Series in Poetry Editor: Jon Tribble**
**Open Competition Award Judge for 2005: Leslie Adrienne Miller**

Library of Congress Cataloging-in-Publication Data

Somers-Willett, Susan B. A., date.
   Roam / Susan B. A. Somers-Willett.
      p. cm. — (Crab Orchard series in poetry)
   I. Title. II. Series: Crab Orchard award series in poetry.
PS3619.O445R63 2006
811'.6—dc22                                            2005027591
ISBN 0-8093-2690-6
ISBN 978-0-8093-2690-7

Printed on recycled paper. ♻

The paper used in this publication meets the minimum requirements of American National Standard for Information Sciences—Permanence of Paper for Printed Library Materials, ANSI Z39.48-1992. ⊛

*For my father, Mark,*

*who taught me I was always free*

*to climb trees*

Abode where lost bodies roam each searching for its lost one.

—SAMUEL BECKETT,

*The Lost Ones*

CONTENTS

# THREE

ACKNOWLEDGMENTS

Grateful acknowledgement is made to the editors of the following journals, where some of the poems in this collection first appeared, sometimes in earlier forms:

*Beloit Poetry Journal*—"Dedications for a Birmingham Clinic"
*Borderlands*—"Virginia Dare" *(i–vi)*
*Connecticut Review*—"*Girl, 7, Seeking U.S. Flight Record, Dies in Crash*"
*Crab Orchard Review*—"The Boy Who Would Be Achilles"
*The Cream City Review*—"Circus Acts": "Ring One, The Magician's Assistant," and "Ring Three, The Lion Tamer"; and "The Naming of Eve"
*Earth's Daughters*—"Ophelia's Technicolor G-String: An Urban Mythology"
*Hayden's Ferry Review*—"A Pain, a Fencepost, a Black-and-White Film"
*iris: a journal about women*—"Heat"
*The Madison Review*—"Circe with Her Hair Down," "Where He Lives Rhymes with Rome," and "Self-Portrait as Interstate 10"
*Midwest Poetry Review*—"September in Ohio"
*RATTLE*—"Notes for Living in NOLA"
*The Saint Ann's Review*—"Cowboys and Indians"
*Spoon River Poetry Review*—"What the Doctors Forget to Tell You about Morphine," "The Gift," "In Memory of a Girl," and "A Note on the Type"

"Notes for Living in NOLA" received an honorable mention for the *Southern California Anthology*'s Ann Stanford Poetry Prize.

"Circe with Her Hair Down," "Where He Lives Rhymes with Rome," and "Self-Portrait as Interstate 10" were awarded the Phyllis Smart Young Poetry Prize.

"The Effects of Light on a Woman's Body" was awarded the Robert Frost Foundation Poetry Award.

I would also like to thank my friends and colleagues who provided me with the personal and professional support needed to complete this book: Craig Arnold, Susan Briante, Mike Henry, Heather Knight, Farid Matuk, Moira Muldoon, Phil Pardi, Bruce Snider, Chris Strickling, Genevieve Van Cleve, Larissa Szporluk, Phil West, the writers and administrators at the James A. Michener Center for Writers and the MA program in Creative Writing at the University of Texas at Austin, the Rude Mechanicals, and the Austin Poetry Slam.

I am also greatly indebted to my mentors and teachers: Tom Cable, Judith Kroll, Deborah Pope, David Wevill, and most especially Michael Adams and Kurt Heinzelman.

I am supremely grateful to Jon Tribble for his careful editorial eye and to Leslie Adrienne Miller for selecting this book for the Crab Orchard Series in Poetry. I am also indebted to Bridget Brown and the rest of the staff of Southern Illinois University Press who ensured that this volume was published with care.

To my family—Ernie Cline, Pat Somers, Stella Somers, and Bill and Louise Willett—I thank you most deeply for your love and unflagging belief, turn by turn.

# ONE

Look homeward Angel now, and melt with ruth.

—JOHN MILTON,

"Lycidas"

# Self-Portrait as Interstate 10

Still, the sky is the great equalizer.
Still, I yawn into the visible: yellow sun,
shack, mountains of uncertain
range. What gives life
are two directions: *to* and *away* like a decisive
heart. The saguaros wave
in the way of surrendering bankers.

What is it to be a sign, a coffee cup,
the grave of a doll's discarded leg?
I end, I begin, I have known death
and have doubled back. I am the last
gas station on its three stilts rising
out of the sea, or the child born there.

To hear the ocotillo burst
into white laughter after rain.
To be the keeper of distances,
defined by landscape and trash.
To the foal of cows in spring
and the crossing corpses of Texas,
I say, *Come unto me. Leave.*

Here a cross marks the earth
where three sisters have buried
their animal. Here the dung of a beast
grows sweet to dry in the sun.
To know not night,
but the fading of a lamp. To live
the constant gray of a bayou.

And here, in L.A., here, in Florida,
here in Lake Charles,
towers of sulfur flicker and that hell
singes its lit *I*'s against the good
white clouds. Here swamp, bay,
monument, tin can with a mouth
ragged as a Southern woman and I
am her spine pressed to the bedsheet.

There is no home, only postcards.
No relationship unmarked by distance.
Of all things, I am the same

photograph taken at different
times of day: me, the lyric
of truck tires in a deluge or
me, those years of dark
water in a plant's heart or

me, that small animal
blooming in a hawk's fist—
not drowning, not waving,
but falling out of the sky.

*Girl, 7, Seeking U.S. Flight Record, Dies in Crash*

Headline from April 12, 1996 *New York Times*

There are things you can put a sound to:
the air's rush through aluminum vents, the catch
of flaps on the wing, ticks of hail, the dead hum
of a magnetic needle pressed past
zero, and in these moments you remember

California, a green alphabet
spilling over Half Moon Bay,
circles of topography, a cloud
in the shape of a hand. In these moments

a woman is typing at her desk, a grandmother
recites a baroque prayer in Spanish,
a teenager refines his second-ever kiss, a man
lights a cigarette in gridlock traffic, and they are

like you, at ordinary ages, practicing
the routine of a blue sky in bad weather,
circling the edge of a century
and trying to stay even. You are seven,

attempting a U.S. flight record, close
to birth, and diving into the earth
like a woman already
forgotten, a girl asking her mother,
*Do you hear the rain?*

## September in Ohio

was like most: tempered
and full of muck. The world itself
stayed round at both ends.
Children imagined war
when there was none.
Rain moved in. The difference

lay interior—some letters
got lost in the white bellies of mail vans,
others were opened and appeared blank.
Houses sighed from the weight
of broken retainers and a wife
pined for her lost breast. Sunlight,
when it came, was so white
it ate itself. I remember days
stayed longer, time splayed
two mean fingers against a red wall.

Outside, raccoons eternally
spat, rolled in root, did their best
to drag a sorry tin of baked Alaska.
Nearly born, I also refused
one life for seconds.

# A Pain, a Fencepost, a Black-and-White Film

> *... pain comes unsharably into our midst as at once that which*
> *cannot be denied and that which cannot be confirmed.*
> —Elaine Scarry

Because pain is not *for* anything,
or *of* it—because objects
will enter the body in different
times, spaces—a man

locks his teeth as history clicks
two thin hands along his spine.
*To hear of someone else's pain*
*is to doubt.* Hiroshima

is a film he saw once and in it,
fishing for explanation, a woman
shows the half of her face
which is gone.

*For one to have pain*
*is to have certainty.* Evidence
walks into a hospital
and sits with its hands

folded on its paper
knee. *Surely this,*
the doctors say, *or this*
*will explain the phenomenon*

of the average man who skimmed
an iron fencepost through his jaw. Months later,
he complains of fits, does not kiss
his wife, feels the ghost of a limb

while sleeping. When asked
what it does, he says, *sometimes*
*it sleeps. Sometimes it feels*
*like a village on fire.*

# Virginia Dare *(i)*

first English child born in the Americas, August 18, 1587

Grandpa White leaves Roanoke as Governor,
his new title shimmering from the teak boat
and a kiss trailing off his good, stiff Puritan
arm. Spain lurks over England. The setting
is historically correct: powder-blue
sea, a white rind of sail, some unknown fish
floating at the hull. Grandpa White leaves Roanoke
as he came to it—a silent island
in a uniform of black waves. Virginia
raises her nine days into a fist and makes
history grabbing her mother's hair,
first Christian of America. Ellinor
twirls a tooled lace hanky: goodbye to Dad.

## Where He Lives Rhymes with Rome

but mostly he calls his house *lions*.
He knows there is a petition out
for his relocation or arrest. *Home*

is the word he uses most when searching
for other words, the bookstore. Days
begin with *um*. The names

of his children sound clear
towns in his head, although incorrect.
He has begun to write things down

as per the doctor's instructions: MARQUEE
is a woman's yellow jacket; the walk sign
at 22nd and Lex FINE INDIAN CUISINE.

His cat remains CAT. His daughter
CLEOPATRA and what was that one,
the gentleman with the thin green tie, OLLIE—

CLEOPATRA AND OLLIE LIVE IN NEW BRUNSWICK
WITH THEIR TWO LOVELY SHOES. He asks
the store clerk for a *silver* and some change

has come upon him, he cannot
quite place it, he remembers
the flowers in his right hand with the note

FOR BRIDGIT which of course
means TRASH ON WEDNESDAY
because everything has been

replaced and the visits
are few, or many, or when the cat
perches on the window and raises his tail.

## Virginia Dare *(ii)*

Grandpa White takes the backwards ride of Virginia
in Ellinor's belly, curled in the sleep cabin,
a father in his daughter's womb. On maps,
clouds perpetually huff across oceans as he lands
half-mad from the salt rattling his lungs.
Sometimes England calls him Governor.
He appears to Parliament as a curious man in black.
He sleeps fortnights on the ship; no one
wants to keep house with him, *curious man.*
Years. Years on the brackish water
and the codfish under his bed turning transparent
eyes at him. The Armada skims
between him and Virginia. He dreams
scenery beyond the powder-blue
drum-smoke of cannons: Virginia is walking
in new leather shoes. Ellinor is following
God faithfully and trade begins.
Ellinor is teaching Virginia to speak.
Virginia knows his name.

# The Naming of Eve

Just one seed for the bushel just
one stem for the nest
just a scratch of meat for the
hunger just one name
for the darkness
inside your mouth
it is night where moss blooms
in cheekfolds, the jaw
slips back, fruit splits
the tongue into two
soft tails whispering *say it*
*dammit say it*—that black
word, my name, the sound
of two vowels
divorced

# Heat

In the summer of wanting a child, what the body remembers
is stepping into a hundred degrees' heat,
the wind an unwelcome warm breath

at the backs of your knees. To think,
this year your posture begins to resemble your mother's,
stooping over the kitchen sink in a T-shirt and no bra,

your breasts pointing towards the drain.
At your age, she already had
a child of three to entertain,

her eye trained to wander and judge
the placement of knives. You are born
in a year she could say she let you live.

In August, the temperature becomes a character
between you and all other people. You
kick off the sheets, and the fan's sweep is only inches.

You visit the park on Sunday afternoons,
revisit the tug in your lungs
when a child falls down and is deciding

whether or not to cry its feral cry.
Her first sobs sound like a shining
knife through an apple: *hot, hot.*

You contemplate getting healthy:
you quit smoking and start again,
you read the backs of packaged foods.

Your lover presses a finger to your lips
and sucks one breast and then the other,
letting them rise. You test your own skin for size.

You explain you have no room in your life
for a child. You explore the terrain of your hip
and you think all of your life is for it. Impatience rests

in your spine before sleep: it is even, like the chirping
nature makes at night; or loud, like the rage
of a motorcycle's gears as it careens between houses, surprising

as static; the sound of it sends organs racing
as your lover's hand rests on the tightness
of your back. What the body remembers is how

the heat fights your tamed hair
into something electric. How all of him
rushes into you in its wild career of light.

# Matins

This day I love that good son
bearing pears and mangoes and limes;
I want to slice fruit for you on Sunday morning,
fruit from which you eat, drink, sing glory.

Bearing pears and mangoes and limes,
I offer you their names while you are still sleeping,
fruit from which you eat, drink, sing glory.
This is not a holy dream of children.

I offer you their names while you are still sleeping—
*manwomanboygirl*, palms pressed in sweat—
this is not a holy dream of children
or a song of lives cut short by the knife.

Man, woman, boy, girl, palms pressed in sweat
they pray in houses, human and small,
or sing of lives cut short by the knife.
My body rises. Blood knows this song.

They pray in houses human and small
while we study the reach of limbs grasping fruit.
My body rises, blood knows this song:
it is a lyric without editor.

While we study the reach of limbs grasping fruit,
the week lies on the calendar, a body—
it is a lyric without editor
and we sing the morning. The first day of

the week lies on the calendar, a body
of soft fruit. My cunt whispers, holy,
and we sing the morning of the first day.
In a sound myth, with a prayer

of soft fruit, my cunt whispers: *holy.*
Bells put tongues to body
in a sound myth, with a prayer.
Your once-child's finger moves on the catch.

Bells put tongues to body
and so the church opens herself;
your once-child's finger moves on the catch
and it proclaims *I will, I won't.*

And so, the church opens herself
like the forked mouth of an adder
and it proclaims *I will, I won't*
for we are at the beginning.

Like the forked mouth of an adder,
I want to slice fruit for you on Sunday morning
for we are at the beginning
and this day I love that good son.

# Virginia Dare *(iii)*

He imagines
his ship pulling from the bay November
after November, but no news returns.
The sea sends back no letters, no belabored notes
folded in bottles and wrapped in black ribbon.
Barnacles collect in white blisters on the ship's ribs.
Grandpa White lobbies for the colony
and wins twenty bolts of sackcloth, boxes of salted beef,
prizes for his dis-ease. God wills people to move.
Unmarked barrels line the skiff and the Spanish drift
back toward the continent, their masts
receding into mist like healing bones.
The sea stiffens into a straight black tarp
from one island to another. Desperate women come,
cook, agree to a journey whose name sounds
like what they lost.

# Dedications for a Birmingham Clinic

To the block which lights up bright pink
in tongues of flame, to the glorious
virgin-white building where the mothers
went in and came out
not mothers—goodbye.
To the high school girls
in the hushed carpool
across county lines:

think good things
of the souls and they will forget
the address and next of kin
you left behind. In the fire,
the smiling black
nurse repeats
your good-enough age.

Goodbye to the sick month
when you walked the hallways
with math books
stabbing your navel.
Goodbye to the blocked
calendar marked in blank code
and the phone call
you made in the night. All
is unrecorded, your looped
signature sings from the registry's
cracked skin. *Shhh*.

The bomb is ticking
in the pen gripped
in the receptionist's left hand,
her quiet white sneaker naps
in the driveway. *Shhh.*
The traffic whispers by on wet pavement,
on the television where the reporter
notes pieces of the clinic
pieces of her white uniform
pieces of the red child
you knew for two months
the bomb is ticking
in your belly   counting
the days   counting the pills
escaping memory
you recognize the blue
tile in the streets   is your first memory
coming to
and coming
to that decision you left
that block
empty as a shoe.

For the daughters who
will wake to the sick visit
of other clinics' pills,
for the mothers who
scoop food off their born
children's mouths,
for the women who
watch the guests of their histories
push
through that
familiar door

it is a dangerous thing
knowing
what we know
we haven't named.

## Two Places Where Danger Lives

Perhaps if one place is in America,
and if it is a town with a lake,
and a mother straps her children into
car seats at the time, perhaps

I will enter the moment
in which she imagines herself alone,
a woman in a popular mythology
watching her car roll off
into that particular silence—

        and if that silence gets
        the best of her, if she slips
        the gearshift to the right notch—
        then

I may appear diving into her
landscape, a waxed vision
in a citizen's view—

one heard about on the evening news,
recounting the cliché
she has stumbled into, this same
mother with a different name—

and still you will know nothing of that room

in which another woman
puts her child to bed, snaps on the nightlight,
begins this writing of her life.

# Virginia Dare *(iv)*

Grandpa White prefers
to sleep outside at night, connecting the larger stars.
He becomes his own man again, lying on his
white, moled back and stabbing the night sky
with a pencil. Virginia will know these
creatures by name: Orion and his
diamond-collared dog, the Seven Sisters
cackling with light. Jeweled daughters floating
in the sway of his view. Astern, two women
are sick. The sea turns its white fists into their bellies;
they begin to sleep.

## Stella Stella

As if the golden wires shared by women
would throw off sparks. We worry rocks,
stalk our mothers' bedrooms.
We wipe the shine on with a cloth.

I've asked my mother's rings and watches
in faded jewelry boxes
for some past I could not name
in its long and awkward birth.

At the kitchen table, she strings
winking necklaces of onyx and quartz:
minerals pressed for answers.
Not that she doesn't love her mother,

but that a dread lives there. Our women
married early, got pregnant soon
and tied their jewelry in skirts
to spite the night's moving.

When they slept, they slept lightly,
listening for the child's cough,
kept journals they later threw
at their husbands or threw away.

At seven, I fingered a silver cross
I bought without permission. At nineteen,
I listened to the glissando of widows' fingers
across whalebone chains, their pendants lost.

They buried their husbands in the way
they knew how. My mother became
the terror of a garnet lost in the sheets
and then the dull glow a cameo,

angelskin cheeks in bas-relief.
As if our wishes for the other
would not soften or bend.
When she left her mother,

it was to Lisbon and Saudi Arabia and short
phone calls made from long distances
she pronounced in native tongues.
Now Stella's breath becomes a filigree

on the telephone, my mother's voice
filling the gaps. We know that
like cops, death clocks
the nearest shining thing.

I imagine my mother coming home
and liberating prized china to the wall.
Or smashing a cookie in her mouth. Or trying
perfume from the law of Victorian bottles

arranged on her mother's vanity.
As if what we take with us
could be weighed
by its dancing in the light.

Walk silent, night.
These are women who pledged
their daughters diamonds.
Yes. Notice our edges.

# What the Doctors Forget to Tell You about Morphine

That you have to reason it out, punching
needles into his dying
flesh, your father, that illusion
of peace with the body.
That you know you are killing him,
left unconscious for hours, his amber urine ticking
in the drip-bag. How he eventually cannot speak
through the bliss, and when he says your name
it sounds like a wet towel.

How he wakes up the neighbors every three hours
with the moan. How the empty syringe
makes you wish for your own relief.
That you have to inject it straight
into his heart, and that makes his eyes smile,
makes them glisten and roll,
and how your love gets replaced

by the fixed drum in his body.
How he looks at you like a God
when you open the vein.
How it makes him feel as if he were flying.
How he is, for a time, an angel.

# TWO

unsignificantly

off the coast

there was


a splash quite unnoticed

this was

Icarus drowning


—WILLIAM CARLOS WILLIAMS,

"Landscape with the Fall of Icarus"

# Migration

*for Ilya Kaminsky*

Look at me. My traveler's speech
thrown into this sun-bleached plaza,
a scattering of birds:
the language of cards peeled from a deck.

My speech a stutter of water
in the fountain the working men drink from,

bowls of stone where the birds drink, where the hard village spires

shiver in their dance with silver coins
of morning light—here, in this city,

my speech fills the birds' bones.
Can you hear it, tumbling pell-mell out of the sky
over the acid flute of altitude, over wind

singing all of your holes?

What is the word that repeats itself inside your body?
The word that lives in your chest,
that chases you into the deaf and repeating sea,

the word you whisper as you desperately
swim to the boat of your human self

and look toward the tan and broken shore,
the ugly shore, my shore, hope
turning its million animal limbs in your lungs,

hope's face inside your face forever turning
to view the only home it has known?

In the sky, which is your country,
so many birds are saying you, saying you.

## What's Left

Your ivory cable sweater, the angle
of a tooth, mortgages, bad advice,
midnight conversations, a ballpoint pen
precariously bearing your name
and junk mail also, notes

indecipherable, seagulls crying
over absences of land,
fast food, worry, a blank
hospital bed, a wife and
your daughter, cancer, laughter.

# The Gift

He was a November boy, sign of Scorpio,
fifteen and with smile like James Dean's.
It was all there for us:
his father gone out for the evening
and a king-sized bed free
and the TV on in the other room
and us so young we could taste each other
sitting five feet apart on the couch.

I had picked him up from school
that afternoon; it was ring day,
and I showed him the clunky gold band in the car.
He said it was beautiful, led my hand
to his mouth and kissed the ring
there on my hand, there in the car,
there at three p.m. on a September afternoon
when I didn't know he was a virgin
and wouldn't learn it for two more years.

I could feel the ghost of his body for days afterwards:
the tattoo of his skin underneath my thigh,
the hair on his belly pricking up
like small fires, the innocent rise
of his hips coming to meet me.
I held the blue cusp of his eyes
between my hands as his head dropped
and his chest shuddered
and things were done
and all that sweet boy could say was
*Thank you, thank you, thank you.*

## Virginia Dare *(v)*

August
lights a finger of land through miles.
Virginia smiles a hard crooked line
of green forest and white rock.
Grandpa White leads a prayer over sackcloth
cots for providence, as governors do.
*Virginia and her new language. Virginia*
*and the glass beads of natives. Virginia and*
Ellinor, his daughter waving hello;
and they *will* wave hello, they will see
the ship painted, bearing their small good names.

# The Boy Who Would Be Achilles

Until there is something spoken there,
the ear appears meaningless,
a white, tooled shell. The smiling face
is delicate, your finger on his picture
is touch, slip away,
like walking wet stone.

*Hero.* If you could say it again,
his name would be
awful, the hardest to remember
at parties. It's hard sometimes, you know,
to look at him the way you do,
in the best graces:

groomed in a school photo, or as the fat baby
industriously at play, or inconsequential
against the backdrop of California.
Remember that sky? He stood between
two houses, head cocked to the left
as he once saw in a film, not shot

    like in that dream you had,
    scalp and bone flapping
    a botched mouth.
    You remember nothing

from that day but that the cat got out
and the toilet kept sighing. He stepped out
to war with his impenetrable body,
some other country, and never returned.
*It's not supposed to be like this*
you think you said—

he was always the dutiful one,
quietly came between his brothers' conflicts
and buried the cat's kill in the yard.
No ordinary creature

could expect his death
sooner than your own
right foot would turn left.
You wish him thin,

out of existence,
the weakest archetype
in your good story.
But then, oh—

      to dip him headfirst in that river,
      make him call your name.

*Amanita virosa*


Did you travel by the small river that was our street
did you hide in the garden waiting for hard rain
are you the knuckles of some immigrant hand
or are you the fruit of neglect
did you fall from the sky

four days after the hurricane you rise
from the hot rotten floorboards
of our good neighbor's house

your tenuous veils lift from under the caps
your waxy cups shine deadly in full sun

part of me believes you
were born on an island exotic
part of me believes
you first bloomed from my father's mouth

you spread your cool wings
on the remnants of house
and when you grow heavy you will drop
and when you grow heavy you will release
your terrible copies

your white name
will tumor in our yard in the moonlight
for years I will dig out your angry buttons
for years I will hold back the hungry dog
for years I will pull your tender bodies up
as you awfully push
through the leaf brush

I live here knowing
there is poison in the wood knowing
there was always poison in the wood

                    overnight
you rise up all over the broken city
you resurrect in numbers and are
most certainly destroying angels

I treasure your weird fruit for hours for hours
singing your brief moist hearts

# Notes for Living in NOLA

Learn to hate the tourists
who booze up, who cruise the one-ways
the wrong way and ask
for the *Café du Monde* the *Jax*
the *Cat's Meow* the *Preservation Hall*—

on Bourbon Street they fall for
*I bet you a dollar I can tell*
*where you got those shoes.*

Sleep till noon, your belly
deep and soft; deal cards
and convince others you
once shot the moon.

Stay above water.
Throw parties when there is weather.
Vacation during Mardi Gras
or do Mardi Gras every other day.

Practice the aesthetics
of getting out of bed,
chasing the cat, the beauty
in wavy views of traffic.
Note the poetics of a
shirt stuck to your back.

Baby, you in jazzland
but don't show the blue
notes, the thin ropes
of hate and self-hate
that hold the place together
that cable the soft banks
that sing red cypress, black wire—
                    here,
murder walks slowly,
demands you hand over
your wallet and things;
don't make no fuss and perhaps
he might pass or ax you
out for a beer.

Cultivate a dull eye
like the black boys on Bourbon
who slide and *clack!* for change,
who *tap! tap!* parabolas, who tack
bottlecaps on their Nikes to jump back
to where someone said
they from.

Acclimate to the smell
of exhaust and the canal.
Pick up the perpetual
gifts of beads and cups that wash
onto your lawn yearlong.
Eat the food you are most afraid of.
Don't drink the water.

Learn to hate the tourists
who rip Mammy's face off the sweet
sweet pralines that mark
their journeys South,
who buy posters of the jazz man
whose pearly teeth match
the whites of his Mac-the-Knife eyes
  (but never go into the park
  named after this man:
  it is dangerous: perhaps
  you will die by that knife).

Find people to love
who tell you suspicious histories.
Wash dishes and know there is no end
to roaches. Celebrate obscure holidays
and master riding a bicycle
with a buzz.

   And this:
daily rain at four, torn green fans
of saw palmetto rapping at the screen,
steam moving from your shoes,
the slip of a cool bottle in hand—
you grip it
just before losing it.

Wake up early for Zulu.
Leave before Rex. Regret
has moved to some other country
so dress, make bets, burn, do nothing.

Get on a bus named *Cemeteries.*
These cemeteries are beautiful things.

# Ophelia's Technicolor G-String: An Urban Mythology

The air tonight is thick as curry;
like every night this summer I could cut it
with my wine glass, spray it with mace.
Over and over it would heal together
like a wound, follow my click and pace of heels
down Conti Street, St. Ann, Bourbon.

Oh Hamlet, if you could see me now
as I pump and swagger across that stage, cape dripping to the floor,
me in three-inch heels and a technicolor G-string—
you would not wish me in a convent.
They've made me a queen here, married me off
to a quarter bag and a pint of gin.

The old men tend bark and splatter, rabid
at each table. I think they stay up all night
just to spite the moon. They bring their diseased
mouths to the French Market in the morning,
sell Creole tomatoes to tourists who don't know
what they are. Each bald head shines plump and red.

It seems like so long ago that I modeled
for those legs outside of Big Daddy's—
the ones over the door that swing *in, out, in, out*—
the sculptor made me painted as Mardi Gras.
I thought you might recognize them if you ever passed
with the boys, parading from Abbey to Tavern,
or think them royal feet in need of slippers.

Someday I expect to find you here,
sitting at the table between the first and second rows,
fingering bones or something worse.
And in the end you will throw me a columbine,
light me a Marlboro and take me to a 24-7 where
jukebox light quivers, makes us as thin as ghosts.

But for now, I will dance for the fat man
who sits in your place and sweats his love for me at 3 a.m.,
because only he knows I am Horatio in drag.

## Who What When

where the black
earth opens in a slack
mouth
    begin when

an eye fists against
the sun and turns
blind with raging
    begin with

who could save her what with
her bright hair swaying
lists without her
name
    begin

in Carolina
is the memory
of a woman with no
    how—

among the rats
and black root
cellars

a rope of skin
tied kin
to bone her

shoulder slept
next to a wandering
eye  witness

to her own fabulous
torture
  *she was my girl*

she was a daughter
from her daughter
was a mother removed
from Georgia

was taken to
Carolina and he
fell in love with her strong
back   when

her mother stayed in
kitchens   forests
swayed in great
directions

she heard in the skins of trees
a drumming
and made nights quicken,
draw out their blades

when he heard her sing
he could not know which curse
he was walking into

she did not know
how sharp the hammer
or the whip
or the prick of snow
against her genitals
in the places she was made to sit

we do not know
much about the woman
except what the trial
recorded
and the nothing
that was left of her back

> *she was my girl*
> *slack as a stalk with no water,*
> *something of him*
> *shifted in her,*
> *his face twisted*
> *in her face when winter*
> *banged at the door*

he thought her beautiful,
his hatred was terrible,
the flames he used to crisp her skin
are the same she cooked with,
he splayed his hand to cup her breast,
he flayed open her back

(as if she were a coin
that admitted him at once
to the dead and the living worlds)

*as the girl*
*was coming out of me,*
*pain entered like an animal*
*whose white teeth*
*I could see in my left eye;*
*I could hear the wild trees*
*chant my name*
*Mira  Mira*

look
where his neck crooked
in the false nimbus of starlight,
where his father shouted
*the fool the fool*

look
at the tree where no plaque
notes his spectacular crime
and no stone bears
her small name

ask what black of a moon
walked through that season
bearing no light

hope that this silence
never once resembles
your life

*my girl, I will tell you everything*

# In Memory of a Girl

Perhaps in ten years I will look at this picture of a girl,
her face twisted across an album page
and say, *not that I didn't know her,*
*but that something in her is dead.*

And not that what is dead will be an innocence, or a hope,
but closer to a thought, a sentence trailing off
between words, a thing half-formed in her body
but still hard, a stone.

Perhaps I will look at this picture and laugh back
at the girl, at her blue-jeaned expression,
at the faint smile caught
between her lips like a lie.

Perhaps it will be that she forgot
her own story, stopped
the language of her name, discovered
the place where laughing began to hurt.

Perhaps I will look at this picture and say,
*this is the face of a girl who thought too much.*
Perhaps it will be that she fell in love
with her own body.

Perhaps, in the end, this picture will remind me
of something else: the tired wheel of a woman's laughter,
a boy's kiss that held no promise, the night the moon spilled
her life on the bedsheets.

And what of her unfinished heart, the history
of her knee, the year she saw her father die?
There is not enough room in the earth to bury
all of this dead reason.

Perhaps the girl is waiting
for someone to tell her this life is not a test.
Perhaps she is tired of her show, the accidental world
of the frame, her grin.

This girl is someone, anyone
who can stand still.
But her arrest cannot break the fact
that she is, all the time, spinning.

Tonight I look at this picture and say,
*this girl is moving from center.*
Perhaps what I want to ask is
*who decides what things will fall off*
   *the end of this world?*

# A Note on the Type

The poems were set on the Linotype in Janson,
long thought to be the work of a Dutchman, Anton Janson,
who was a practicing type founder in Leipzig
during the late half of the seventeenth century.
However, it has been conclusively demonstrated

that these types were actually the work of another man,
a Hungarian, who learned his trade from another man,
a Dutchman, who himself was responsible
for training many such men in a basement

and who was born of a woman and man
who also had mothers and fathers and birthplaces
whose names did not survive

but note how the sturdy faces
stand from the page
and how important the family
has become to us, coming to us
through the incomparable design
of a tree's white
breath

# Virginia Dare *(vi)*

No smoke or signs of settlement. No
tree whispers a secret. The white pines jack
at a powder-blue sky with no Roanoke
to govern. A post hisses CROATOAN
but there are no crosses waving. Trees cross
and tangle like Ellinor's black hair.
The shore of Virginia smiles her rock-toothed grin
and is three years old. Grandpa White begins

to disappear. His hair recedes in a dark
accent of bone. Ash marks the days he is
gone, then snow. White trees starve at intervals,
wave hello and goodbye. The women
speculate, are sick, give birth to his side
of the world. *Where has she gone,* they ask,
*daughter of John the Governor,* the man
*at whom fish rolled their terrible eyes?*

They talk of this country, how
it is beginning to eat its people.

## Cowboys and Indians

I was the cowboy, and pointing
a stick at you said *bang*.
You refused to be dead.

You ran around the yard half-naked
patting your mouth like a native.
I continued to kill you
until the end of the game.

Then we traded weapons
and I smeared the war paint
onto my own nude body like a target.

You wore a hat. I wore a skin.

# The Effects of Light on a Woman's Body

after *Overflow* by Andrew Wyeth

This afternoon, while picking blackberries,
Helga noticed the silence of birds in the painter's presence
even after a time, as if listening to his brushstrokes

were a careful language one could hear only
in utter stillness. Today she thinks perhaps *she* is a bird,
for she knows the soft stutters of horsehair on paper

are followed by the slop of water in a jar, knows
the sounds of the brush's handle ringing the glass rim like a bell
and the brush wrung of its dirty water: a sentence made of light.

Light meditating on her body before moving on
for the trees or evening, light moving in and speaking her,
his water still for a time and then poured away—

these effects from which might appear her eyes
cradled in the rose-colored slings of her lids,
her eyes averted or closed, as if seeing weren't seeing at all

but instead the product of an inner music, his seeing
a note played back and forth across the page.
This is why, while her breath makes the pattern of resting,

her woman's body listens—*still here, still here*—
so to hear the dry tool make its points as she reclines,
her breasts flattening into pear-shaped pools his brush dips into,

the tender boat of her genitals floating
in her own wild patch of blonde reeds. In her dreams
there is always this dark water stirring,

water which would never think to be silent,

water which is the praise of his voice.

# The Boxer's Wife

As the boxer shakes fire
from his palsied claw, she is thinking
what they can do to a man.

She is thinking of that woman
she knows will ring for the third time tonight,
who will ask for change, who will

clasp a paper with an apartment's address,
who will rasp through the intercom
*rape* and *doctor*

and from the dark stories
her mother will throw fists of change
at that woman like hard rain.

She is thinking this could be her,
other than herself; she has felt
this way, desperate, searching the floor

for the flash of an earring,
or a shard of glass, or something else
knocked out of her and lost in this country.

The anthem plays
of her man who was once
his own nation, the gothic measures

squawking lost glory through the television
with the black and white pictures
of Cassius kissing his wife and children.

Or that black man bearing his fists
to doctors and presidents. Or that bad poet in Africa
who narrowly missed the boat

of his own undoing. And now here,
Atlanta is burning, the light of sky
is falling; she is thinking

of the sting of his hand.
The geography of his face shifts
in the torch glow, broken light upon bone.

She is thinking: let him remember love
in the slow jag of his fingers along her back,
the high bridge of his neck

rising to meet her neck and their breath
indelible like the gentle
whorl of his thumb to the light's grip.

She is thinking he will fight
with everything in his body
the sad legacy you give him tonight.

# Circus Acts

It opens with a box and an ounce of belief.
The magician enters, throwing his cape to the air.
His assistant, my grandmother, swaggers in

through a backdrop of elephants and the solid
ribs of drums, her staggered walk a sexpot's or invalid's,
her tired arm thrown out to the crowd in a wave.

She has studied the cracks in silver rings, learned
to disappear in a moment of silence, how to keep birds
quiet while caged. And at the man's command,

she enters the box and is ready to be divided
into parts one, two, and three. She wiggles her toes
as he brandishes the saw. Then the man

becomes a surgeon cutting off her breast.
It is the same man, blade, box, crash of cymbals,
but she has forgotten the trick. She does not let on

to her fear or the fact of her body, cut.
We whistle and cheer, assuring her
it's all done with mirrors. Observe

this woman in a box, the immaculate glove
splayed over her body for praise.
She pulls it off, all belief and too much lipstick.

RING TWO

THE TIGHTROPE WALKER

My mother steps off
one end of the platform,
through the unknown weight of air
to that place where everything
must stop, wire
shifting violently, wire
middling through skin.
This is where she is made

to begin. She feels the chill of balance
in her belly, her chest, her outstretched arms
stray compass needles
she cannot follow, right foot
brushing nothing, left
feeling the quick sink
of bones to the line.

As if the wire will divide
her body in two.

As if she is at once
the woman paused in mid-air
and her dead twin below.

She must find that link
of one half to the other,
make the desperate shift to center.
In the awe of her walking,
voices of both spring from the rope:
*Gravity will kill you.*
*Gravity is what keeps you here.*

RING THREE

THE LION TAMER

It's not that I like being in the pit,
or standing in the center ring, or shoving my head
into a lion's mouth. It's as simple as this:

woman tames lion or lion eats woman.
It's not a matter of flesh, but the breath
I smell every day, looking into that animal,

that waft of old food and piss.
There's a constant suspense
between the jaw and the body, between

the tests of these things I know:
in one hand, the whip; in the other,
a hoop of fire. Learning to live

with the cat and his props.
Teaching him the difference
between me and some other meat.

# Circe with Her Hair Down

How beautiful to kiss him on that edge
of soda and Jack, his hand over the glass
like an old cat on a top limb

arching its five hairs toward his lives.
His tongue forgets itself.
The teeth forget their days

and twenties in the sock drawer.
His lips are two cracked moons
drowning in the hotel sink he stares into.

Soon his leg curves to your
ankle in bed and his foot
takes the shape of a lobster's hook.

The face he makes while sleeping
resembles his house and his clothes thrown
on the darkening lawn.

He could be falling through water
with his hair this way,
at war with gravity—

with the dead-man float of his limbs
on these gray sheets—
master of the slow drift

away from himself. He kisses his boy's photo
and in moments, he is a continent
and you an adulteress.

You learn to love
the smell of other wives
on his fingers, the foreign stitch

of war wounds. His dog
retches in his kidney.
The link fence sings

and is not unlike his ribs.
You conjure an island, shake the bad rain
from your head, and still

          a sea collects in the bathtub,
          all his former addresses
                    erased—

and the body is here
because it cannot retrieve where
it wants to go, to whom. Comb

his hair and he assumes
you are a woman willing
to live in this country.

# пустота (Emptiness)

*After us there will be emptiness.*

—Irina Vizovkin, one of two remaining citizens

of Lebyazhy, Russia

I lift full pails of water from our well with one arm
I lift them without leaning over
I busk them across the land

I am the strong one standing in wheatgrass
I steady the water
your granny could not do this

Vitaly throws sacks of red potatoes in the tractor
he throws grain to the rooster and studies the grass
he sharpens the blade of the gut knife for dinner
and I kill the weak one, the slow-moving calf

his throat moves against itself as it empties
it sounds like the relief of a rainstorm
it sounds like a mouth with no voice

sometimes in winter our gate sings
with ice, I can see the tracks of rodents
as if they were breaths in the snow
and I can talk to the bird in the hard tree
across the row
he is a blackbird, I can talk to him
if I can see him

the man who lived
in the town next to ours
had no one to bury him
and so we brought him over and covered his door
and so my address is
*woman with the scrap tractor who lives with her husband*
*next to the town whose people*
*have been erased*

in winter the water must be knocked from the well
in winter the water must be wrung out of ice
and I do

Vitaly asks if he will die like the man in Vershina
if he will have to be buried over distance, if he will have to be found
I tuck the chicken's legs under her pimpled belly
I bury the bread dough into its pan
days go on without us
saying such things

this week I buy kerosene from the traveling store
Lebyazhy has been lifted from the map
but the store finds us
it arrives on Tuesdays at a certain time
and I sit on my bench hours beforehand
and I sit on my bench hours beforehand

and the white truck chuffs its way
up our road which is sometimes brown,
sometimes white, sometimes overgrown

sometimes the truck comes panting like Vitaly
sometimes the truck comes not at all

I talk to the moose if I can see
the gleaming velvet of their antlers in daylight
the father's antlers sound a rifle shot when they hit the gate
and the young one's look like the soft tips of corn

I lift full pails of water from our well
when I carry the pail, the water slops
where I roam the water forms a mouth

on Sundays I wash the graves and pick the moss off
the name of the man from Vershina
I wring the chicken and watch her neck slowly unwind
when I carry the water in the pail it talks to me

in autumn I talk to the foxes
who chase the wire of our broken gate
they are here if I can see them
they are red and hot
in their circling of us

it is summer, we watch each other,
we work and are thirsty, I grasp the pail of water
full and white-knuckled, as if I am shaking a hand

# After Leaving the House of Minos

Oh gust of wind, jasmine riding
your airy hooks to reach me even at this height,

generous wind with your sharp and searching fingers:
bring my boy back to me.

Fish him out of the sea, instill
in him your brine-full breath,

reverse his terrible descent
and place him next to me in the sky

as a bright bird or a wild, pointed star.
He grows sour in the partnering waves;

dark water, spit him back and I will catch him,
I will discover the right magic

to make his life happen if it were only
for the sea's release. Hear the crash of him calling,

asking. Here my desire repeats
as it will always repeat, living as it does

in my saline blood, in my sleep-ill dreams
where the dead visit to speak:

*I did not die, it was a mistake;*
*you threw the wrong body to the wind.*

My boy, this heart is an ear listening for you.
Every day I wish you back onto shore,

into me; every dreaming night I look down
to the memory of you—a shining

small thing in the nightscape of water
as men of war glow and tumor the sea—

and this night I bless you, I bless you there
watching me hang winged and alive

in the sky of my mind,
I bless your boy's eyes in their knowing.

# THREE

There are many kinds of open

how a diamond comes into a knot of flame

how sound comes into a word, coloured

by who pays what for speaking.

—AUDRE LORDE,

"Coal"

# Jeanne's Memory

In response to her inquisitors

It is all about climbing
that tree, the one arm
over the other, the weird work
of joining words to a scene:

myself, in a slash of color
where there once was none, conjuring
people in a white field and adding
shrubbery, births, the slap of tongues,
textures of rain. No:

*I never saw any fairies under the tree*
*to my knowledge.* As I say this,

all of Domrémy spools out
from a bald forest where witches,
by legend, inhabited the gaps.
What else is there to remember?
The tree was already half underground.

I produce girls moving
through the brown landscape of another location,
a white sky which passes
in the wrong direction. Yes,
*I may have danced there sometimes*
*with the children; but I sang there*
*more than danced.* I go back

to some beginning, touching the skins
of the things laid out for display, my feet
still, moving, still wedged to earth.
As if nothing else is important
except what the world imagines
to flash in great detail and be gone.
Perhaps *I have seen girls*
*hang wreaths on the branches;*

*and sometimes we took them away with us*
*and sometimes we left them behind.*

# Jeanne Crosses

Moving across the border,
one word becomes another.
My name is not Jeanette, meaning my father's pet,
but Jeanne, meaning woman whom the Lord has favored.
I make this up as I go along.

I ride in the cart with the books, iron kettles,
wooden dolls whose limbs
knock out the noise of crickets.
*My mother had told me that my father often dreamed*
*I would run away with a band of soldiers.*
I ride with the sick, the out of luck,
the pale woman who gave birth
and died, the furry horseflies that bite
and bite. The drivers mumble into the air—
men who see a road
unfolding in the dark—

and I tell them my woman's name,
that I was sent for,
I am fed and given hay for a bed,
I bring nothing on this journey
but myself:
       a child *from my mother*
       *I learned Our Father,*
       *Hail Mary, and I believe.*

The pink baby wrinkles endlessly.
The dead woman begins to reek
although I bless her over and over again.
I see my child's days open
in toothless mouths of light:

the flash of silvery wood in water meets
the churning of wings across sky.
Wash day. The sun is God's mouth.
The skin the clothes make as I push them down
makes a cry. That could be my head.
*My father said that if his dream came to pass,*
*he would want my brothers to drown me,*
*and if they refused, he would drown me himself.*

Oh woman, bad nurse
whose right hand I circled at the church—
eyeless woman, faceless woman, bright
as the ring of white around blood on nuptial sheets—
why did I take your mouth, rise, raise the siege?

Catherine, you were worse than any room
I could have walked into.

## Jeanne Sleeping

*I do not know A from B.*
Sleep is a ghost made of
other people's clothes.
In one dream, I lead.
In one dream, I pass playhouses
to loot trash barrels, and move beyond
calling. In one dream,

iron sings on an anvil like a traveler.
A bitch circles the town and cannot find
her pups. Prostitutes laugh with their guts
slung over wood terraces, and black flies
suckle their rutted necks. *As for other*
*womanly duties, there are enough*
*other women to perform them.*
In one dream, God

puts his back to the earth in a flax field
and sleeps, his hair smelling of
blackroot and piss. The scarecrow there
points in two directions:
Here. Here. Here.

# Jeanne in the Country of Lost Things

Where I go when I enter battle
is where the breaths of other people
lean in wait against gray skies and we use sieves
to capture rain. In the farmlands,
the plains crack for lack of being walked upon;
birds search for greener terrain
and the glint of something man-made.

In the city, keys sing from clotheslines.
The clothes have blown to forests. From a distance,
you can hear the jingle of angles meeting
which is not unlike the flapping of wings.
Closer, they sound like church bells
stuck in one continuous ring. How all of them shine
over the piles of wedding bands.

In the streets of the city,
children cling to the edges of coats
they believe to be their mothers'.
A calico paces circles
around a limp mouse—or is it
a child's toy, or a brown sock

sucked into this country by God's breath
and which he now calls his own?
The volume of monocles
take up states and shatter themselves
in the sun out of little patience.

Where I go is the country
where baby teeth line the beach
and click under the heels of dogs wandering,
where strays waul into dimly lit corners,
where homes groan from the weight of empty rooms,
where mothers cry *oh* into their children's red coats,
where the waves crest and crash
like words said in anger—

      you cannot take them back—

where I lean against the hissing
backdrop of generic trees and sky,
where dim stars beat out their lives
next to those that were never missed—

where I go is this country
where I search for the family songbird,
a favorite knife, the story
that took place over two years,
a secondhand boy's breastplate,
and you, yes father, you.

## Jeanne in the Presence of Instruments

The rack, the screw,
the hook with pointed end and eye,
smoldering sticks, cloth in oil,
the jag of an old man's tooth,
the stake, an arm of rope,
the crushing hammer and the claw,
the wooden yolk, horses
sent in different directions,
rocks dashed to the head and some to the sky,
recitation of saints most would not remember,
skin stripped from the body,
public inquisition,
the strong man and his pick, fire:
these are what little girls are made of.

I am threatened with torture
in the presence of instruments.
I confess: the truth is
not the story you've heard of that sorry girl
or the virago, the bad haircut done on the fly,
not the men I supposedly loved or the women,
their delicate organs curling inside,
not the dumb soul rising upward
in its pitiful tube. It's this:

I expected celebrations in the name of the King
but also in mine. I attest
I am a vain girl, that my father
wanted to kill me by drowning, that my god
lost his temper and I

practiced the dark law of a soldier.
That a woman spoke to me
and said I must deliver this world,

and I desired it, I felt my legs
and they became possible,
my knee bent tensile, wound
like the gut, and I declared too

my beautiful world haunted,
my heart has chanted:
*I want, I want.*
I am threatened as if my body

weren't already confirmed, earthbound,
powder strewn across the happy sky.

The tools make no difference.
Where I fly is limitless.

"A Pain, a Fencepost, a Black-and-White Film": The epigraph and the lines "To hear of someone else's pain is to doubt" and "For one to have pain is to have certainty" are quoted from Elaine Scarry's *The Body in Pain: The Making and Unmaking of the World* (New York: Oxford University Press, 1985).

"Who What When": According to North Carolina state court records, slave owner John Hoover systematically tortured his slave Mira from December 1838 until her death on March 27, 1839. During this period, she was in the later stages of pregnancy and gave birth to a child, perhaps Hoover's. Her torture reportedly consisted of beatings with chains, whips, clubs, sticks, braces; being chained at the neck to a log; being forced to sit in a pile of snow with her genitalia exposed, so as to induce abortion; sexual abuse; and the burning of parts of her body with open flames. The back of the corpse was described as "a continuous wound . . . a perfect skeleton" from which strips of skin six inches to a foot long fell. It appears that John Hoover was the only slave owner ever hanged in the South for killing a slave. See "In Remembrance of Mira: Reflections on the Death of a Slave Woman" by Carolyn J. Powell in *Discovering the Women of Slavery: Emanicpating Perspective on the American Past*, edited by Patricia Morton (University of Georgia Press, 1996). *Mira* is Spanish for the imperative form of "to look."

The Jeanne D'Arc poems: The italicized lines of this series are from Joan of Arc's trial, conducted by the Catholic church, as published in *Joan of Arc in Her Own Words*, compiled and translated by Willard Trask (New York: Books and Company/Turtle Point Press, 1996).